This book

Welcome!

We hope you are ready to laugh non-stop!

In a moment, you will find the funiest Valentine's Day jokes that you can share with your friends and family.

We hope you have fun and get unlimited laughs!

CHAPTER 1

Knock Knock Jokes

Happy Valentine's Day! Knock, knock.

Who's there?

Howard.

Howard who?

Howard you like to be my Valentine?

Hello again! Knock, knock.

Who's there?

Olive.

Olive who?

Olive you!

Knock Knock. Who's there?

Bea.

Bea who?

Bea my Valentine!

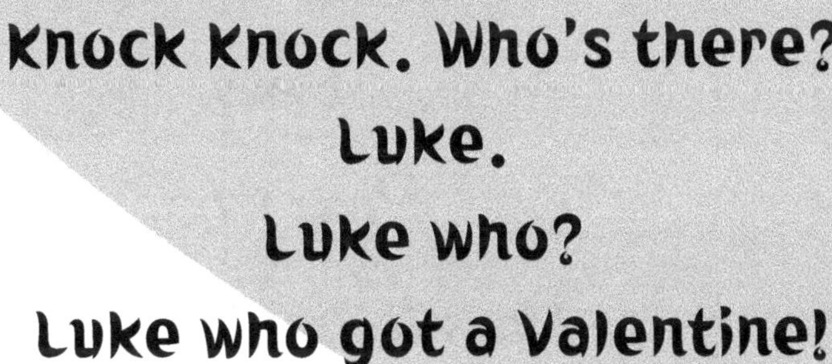

Knock Knock. Who's there?

Luke.

Luke who?

Luke who got a Valentine!

Knock, knock. Who's there?

Arthur.

Arthur who?

Arthur any chocolates left for me?

Knock, knock. Who's there?

Peas.

Peas who?

Peas be my Valentine!

Knock, knock. Who's there?

Al.

Al who?

Al be your Valentine if you'll be mine.

Knock, knock! Who's there?

Jamaica.

Jamaica who?

Jamaica me a Valentine?

Knock, knock! Who's there?

Luke.

Luke who?

Luke, I got you a Valentine!

Knock, Knock! Who's there?

Eye

Eye who?

Eye want to wish you
a Happy Valentine's Day!

Knock Knock. Who's there?
Justin.
Justin time to give you a Valentine.

Knock, knock! Who's there?
Will.
Will who?
Will you be my Valentine?

Knock, knock. Who's there?

Ima.

Ima who?

Ima hoping you will be my Valentine!

Knock, knock. Who's there?

Donut.

Donut who?

Donut you know I love you!

Knock, knock! Who's there?

Tail.

Tail who?

Tail all your friends Happy Valentine's Day!

Knock, knock! Who's there?

Sherwood.

Sherwood who?

Sherwood like to be your valentine!

Knock Knock. Who's there?

Needle.

Needle who?

Needle little love.

Knock Knock. Who's there?

Honeydew.

Honeydew who?

Honeydew you want to be my Valentine?

Who's there?

Jimmy.

Jimmy who?

Jimmy a hug! It's Valentine's Day.

Knock Knock. Who's there?

Kiss

Kiss who?

Kiss me!

Knock, knock. Who's there?

Frank.

Frank who?

Frank you for being my friend!

love

Knock Knock. Who's there?

Arthur.

Arthur who?

Arthur any Valentine chocolates for me?

Knock, knock. Who's there?

Howard

Howard who?

Howard you like a big hug?

Who's there?

Iguana.

Iguana who?

Iguana hold your hand.

Knock, knock! Who's there?

Mary.

Mary who?

Mary me, I love you!

Knock, knock! Who's there?

Adore.

Adore who?

Adore stands between us, open the door!

Knock, knock! Who's there?

Parmesan.

Parmesan who?

Do I have parmesan to take you to the Valentine's dance?

Knock, knock! Who's there?

Joanna.

Joanna who?

Joanna be my Valentine?

Knock, knock! Who's there?

Raisin.

Raisin who?

You're the raisin I'm so happy.

Knock, knock! Who's there?

Owl.

Owl who?

Owl always love you.

Knock, knock! Who's there?

Fondue.

Fondue who?

I'm very fondue you.

Knock, knock! Who's there?

Frank.

Frank who?

Frank you for loving me.

CHAPTER 2

Q&A Jokes

Q: What does Cupid always have with his pizza?

A: Wings.

Q: Who is Cupid's favorite superhero?

A: The Arrow.

Q: What is Cupid's favorite rock band?

A: Heart

Q: What indoor sport does Cupid play?

A: Darts.

Q: How do you dish out ice cream of Valentine's Day?

A: You sCupid out.

Q: Which football team does Cupid cheer for?

A: The Dolphins.

(Cupid is often shown riding dolphins)

Q: Who does Cupid send a Valentine to using twitter?

A: His tweetheart.

Q: What Valentine's Day candy does Cupid like most?

A: Hershey's Kisses.

Q: Which English city does Cupid like most?

A: Loverpool.

Q: Why is lettuce Cupid's favorite vegetable?

A: Because it's got heart.

Q: Why didn't Cupid make it to the Valentine's Day party on time?

A: He was ChocoLATE

Q: What did Cupid name his pet pig?

A: Valenswine.

Q: What card game can you never beat Cupid at?

A: Hearts

Q: What do you call the Pigeon god of love?

A: Coo-pid.

Q: What did the cook say to his girlfriend?

A: You're bacon me crazy!

Q: What did one lightbulb say to the other on Valentine's Day?

A: I love you watts and watts.

Q: What kind of flower do you never give on Valentine's Day?

A: Cauliflower.

Q: What did the refrigerator say to the magnet?

A: I find you very attractive.

Q: How did the doorbell propose to his sweetheart?

A: He gave her a ring.

Q: What did the volcano say to his mother?

A: I lava you.

Q: Why didn't the skeleton want to celebrate Valentine's Day?

A: His heart wasn't in it. Tee-hee!

Q: What did the whale say to his sweetheart on Valentine's Day?

A: Whale you be mine?

Q: What did the squirrel say to his mate?

A: I'm nuts about you.

Q: Why are flowers popular on Valentine's Day?

A: Because they're scent-imental!

Q: What did the kitten say on Valentine's Day?

A: You're purr-fect.

Q: What did the stamp say to the envelope on Valentine's Day?

A: I'm stuck on you!

Q: What do you call the world's smallest Valentine's Day card?

A: A Valen-teeny.

Q: Why did the sheriff lock up her boyfriend?

A: He stole her heart.

Q: What did the cucumber say to his friend?

A: You mean a great dill to me.

Q: What did one bee say to the other?

A: I love bee-ing with you, honey.

Q: What do you say to a spider on Valentine's Day?

A: I want to hold your hand, hand, hand, hand, hand, hand, hand, hand!

Q: What did Frankenstein's monster say to his bride on Valentine's Day?

A: Be my Valen-stein!

Q: What did the painter say to her sweetheart?

A: I love you with all my art.

Q: Do you have a date for Valentine's Day?

A: Yes! It's February 14th.

Q: What did one pie say to the other?

A: Pie like you berry much.

Q: What type of shape is most popular on Valentine's Day?

A: Acute triangle.

Q: What did one light bulb say to the other on Valentine's Day?

A: "I love you a whole watt."

Q: What did the needle say to the thread?

A: You're sew special to me.

Q: What did the tree say to the houseplant?

A: Do you beleaf in love?

Q: What did the scientist say to his sweetheart?

A: We've got good chemistry.

Q: What did one flame say to the other on Valentine's Day?

A: "We're a perfect match!"

Q: What did one blueberry say to the other on Valentine's Day?

A: "I love you berry much."

Q: What did the dustpan say to the broom?

A: You sweep me off my feet!

Q: What did the one sheep say to the other?

A: I love ewe!

Q: What do you call a ghost's true love?

A: Their ghoul-friend.

Q: What did one watermelon say to the other on Valentine's Day?

A: "You're one in a melon!"

Q: Where do all the hamburgers take their girlfriends on Valentine's Day?

A: To a meatball.

Q: What do you write in a slug's Valentine's Day card?
A: Be my Valen-slime!

Q: Why is Valentine's Day a good day for a party?
A: Because you can really party hearty!

Q: What do you call two birds in love?
A: Tweethearts!

Q: What did the rabbit say to his girlfriend on Valentine's Day?

A: "Somebunny loves you!"

Q: "What does a carpet salesman give his wife for Valentine's Day?"

A: "Rugs and kisses."

Q: What did the farmer give his wife for Valentine's Day?

A: Hogs and kisses.

Q: What flower gives the most kisses on Valentine's Day?

A: Tu-lips.

Q: What shade of red is your heart?

A: Beat red!

Q: What's red on the outside and has you on the inside?

A: My heart. Ba-dum-bump!

Q: What did one Jedi say to the other on Valentine's Day?

A: Yoda one for me!

Q: Why would you want to marry a goalie?

A: Because he (or she) is a real keeper!

Q: Why are artichokes so beloved?

A: They're known for their hearts.

Q:Why is lettuce the most loving vegetable?

A: Because it's all heart.

Q: What did the chef give to his wife on Valentine's Day?

A: A hug and a quiche.

Q: "What did the snake say to his girlfriend on Valentine's Day?"

A: "Give me a little hiss."

Q: What did one piece of toast say to the other?

A: "You're my butter half!"

Q: What did the Valentine get arrested for?

A: For stealing someone's heart.

Q: What did the baker say to his sweetheart?

A: "I'm dough-nuts about you!"

Q: What did one watermelon say to the other on Valentine's Day?

A: You're one in a melon!

Q: What did one sheep say to the other sheep on Valentine's Day?

A: I love you baaaaaaaaa...ck.

Q: What did the ghost say to his wife on Valentine's Day?

A: "You look so BOOtiful."

Q: Who always has a date on Valentine's Day?

A: A calendar.

Q: "Why is lettuce the most loving vegetable?"

A: "Because it's got heart."

Q: "Why did the man send his wife a tweet on Valentine's Day?"

A: "Because she is his tweetheart!"

Q: Why did the boy and girl play tennis on their date?

A: It was a court-ship.

Q: How does cupid visit his girlfriend?
A: "On an arrow-plane!"

Q: What did the bat say to his girlfriend?
A: You're fun to hang around with.

Q: What did the calculator say to the pencil on Valentine's Day?

A: "You can always count on me."

Q: What did the drum say to the other drum on Valentine's Day?

"My heart beats for you."

Q: How can you tell the calendar is popular?
A: It always has a lot of dates.

Q: What did the elephant say to his girlfriend?
A: I love you a ton!

Q: What happens when you fall in love with a French chef?

A: You get buttered up.

Q: What did the dolphin do when his girlfriend broke up with him?

A: He whaled.

Q: "What did pilgrims give each other on Valentine's Day?"
A: "Mayflowers"

Q: Why did the bee marry the rabbit?
A: She was his honey bunny.

Q: What do you call romance in a fish tank?

A: Guppy love.

Q: What did one marshmallow say to the other?

A: I want s'more time with you!

Q: "Why did the boy have his girlfriend put in jail?"
A: "She stole his heart."

Q: What did A send B on Valentine's day?
A: A love letter.

Q: What happend when the cow didn't get any Valentines?

A: She felt mooooo-dy

Q: What did the chocolate syrup say to the ice cream on Valentine's day?

A: I'm sweet on you.

Q: Why did the boy put candy under his pillow?

A: Because he wanted sweet dreams.

Q: What do cows like to do on Valentine's day?

A: Cud-dle.

Q: What did the bear say to his sweetie on Valentine's day?

A: I love you bear-y much.

Q: How did the farmer show his wife he loved her?

A: He brought home the bacon.

Q: What did the girl snake say to the boy snake?

A: Will you be my boa-friend?

Q: What do bunnies do when they get married?

A: They go on a bunny moon.

Q: Why did the cats get married?

A: Because they are purrrr-fect to each other.

LOVE
is
LOVE

www.ingramcontent.com/pod-product-compliance
Lightning Source LLC
LaVergne TN
LVHW052101160826
845678LV00015B/3313

* 9 7 9 8 4 1 6 7 7 7 9 7 5 *